Mega Mazes

Rolf Heimann

Sterling Publishing Co., Inc.

NEW YORK

Library of Congress Cataloging-in-Publication Data Available

2 4 6 8 10 9 7 5 3 1

Published by Sterling Publishing Co., Inc.
387 Park Avenue South, New York, NY 10016
© 2006 by Rolf Heimann
This edition is excerpted from material originally published in Australia
under the titles *Amazing Mazes*, *Amazing Mazes 2*, and *Amazing Mazes 3*
copyright © 1989, 1994, and 1996 by Rolf Heimann
Published by arrangement with Roland Harvey Books,
Port Melbourne, Australia
Distributed in Canada by Sterling Publishing
c/o Canadian Manda Group, 165 Dufferin Street
Toronto, Ontario, Canada M6K 3H6

Printed in China
All rights reserved

Sterling ISBN 13: 978-1-4027-2461-9
ISBN 10: 1-4027-2461-6

For information about custom editions, special sales, premium and
corporate purchases, please contact Sterling Special Sales Department
at 800-805-5489 or specialsales@sterlingpub.com.

Contents

Amazing History

The world's most famous maze is without a doubt the labyrinth of ancient Minoan mythology. It was built by Daedalus to imprison the Minotaur, a man-eating monster. Whoever entered the labyrinth could abandon all hope of ever finding the way out. People were forced into its dark passages to be devoured by the Minotaur as human sacrifices.

The Athenian prince, Theseus, finally volunteered to be sacrificed, secretly planning to slay the monster. He succeeded in doing so and even found his way out with the aid of a long thread given to him by Ariadne, the king's daughter who had fallen in love with Theseus.

The story is, of course, a legend. But archaeologists were surprised when they excavated the ruins of Minoan palaces in the island of Crete. The intricate layouts of these palaces—some with as many as 1,500 rooms—reminded them of mazes.

Many civilizations throughout the ages used mazes, usually for amusement. Even today we have fairgrounds that feature mirror mazes and people pay good money for the fun of getting lost! Modern scientists use mazes as part of intelligence tests for animals, as well as for people.

Hundreds of years ago, architects often incorporated maze designs in the decoration of churches and other buildings. They looked upon these designs, with their confusing paths and many dead ends, as symbols of our journey through life. How often we are in doubt about which path to take! Sometimes it is only a lucky guess that puts us on the right track. But even if we meet one dead end after another, we must not get disheartened.

Lila, Tom, and Ben are confronted by all sorts of mazes in this book. Some are very easy and some are quite difficult. Lila is the oldest and will attempt the hardest ones. Ben, the youngest, will do the easiest ones, while Tom goes for those in between.

1. The Labyrinth

Lila, Tom, and Ben are visiting a film studio—and what a thrill it is! Tom recognizes the famous film star Miss Lemour and asks for her autograph.

"Sure honey," she says, "but be a darling and plug in my hair dryer. It must be one of those cables over there . . ."

Miss Lemour hasn't even noticed that her poodle, Fifi, has wandered off onto the film set. Ben discovers Fifi but can't reach her, even when he stands on the sign. Will the dog be able to get back to where the ladder leans against the wall?

In the meantime, Lila hears distressed calls from two workmen who have been putting finishing touches to the Minotaur's Maze. Now they can't find their way out!

From the top of the ladder Lila should be able to guide them back.

Solution on page 72

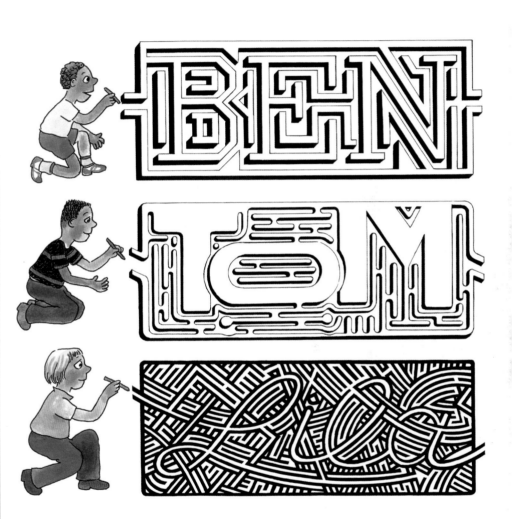

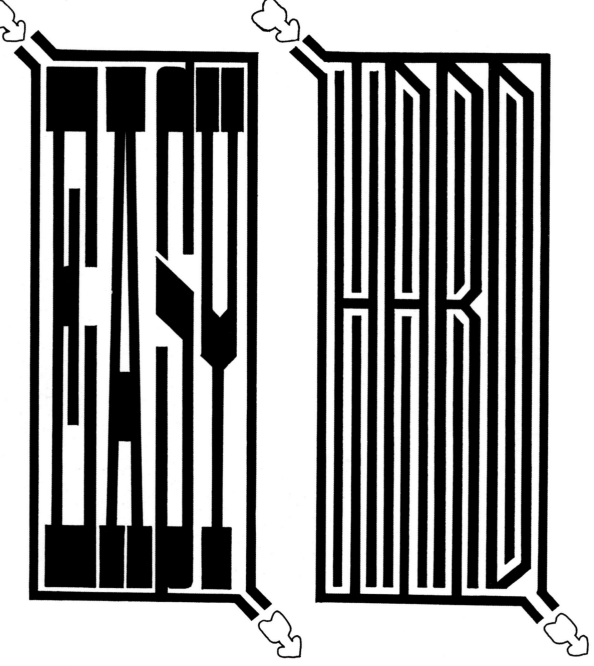

Dazzling Duet

See if you can make your way out of these mazes
in less than 90 seconds.

2. Drinks in the Pipeline

Lila, Tom, and Ben are thirsty. There are three glasses near the lower tanks. But what sort of juice do these tanks hold? The children will have to work it out by following the pipes. Ben likes orange juice, Tom wants lime, and Lila feels like some lemonade.

Solution on page 72

Here's a hint, Lila: when you come to a junction, go with the even numbers...

3. Professor McQueen's Breakfast Machine

Professor McQueen is an inventor who wants to make housework easier. At the moment he is tinkering with a machine that pours the tea and adds milk and sugar. He is very proud of his invention.

But maybe he got a bit carried away this time. He can't even remember which lever operates what and whether he is to push or to pull. In desperation he asks Lila to check his patented sugar dispenser, Tom has to work out how the milk is added, and Ben must check the tea-pouring mechanism.

Solution on page 72

10

4.   Matching Socks

Now that they have finished the washing, Ben, Tom, and Lila have to find their way to the clothesline so that they can match up their socks. Start on the white platform where the odd socks are lying.

Solution on page 72

Solution on page 71

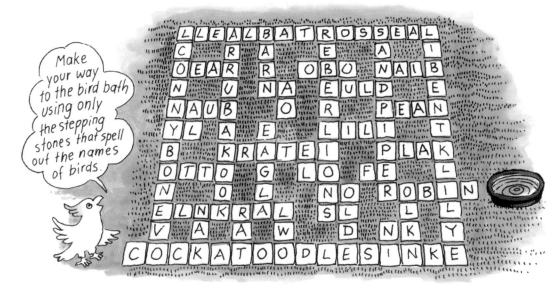

Solution on page 71

5.　Puzzling Picnic

Ben, Tom, and Lila have climbed the lookout tower to check the park's layout before setting out to buy a few more things for their picnic on the lawn.

Ben decides to take the blue boat to buy some apples, while Tom will take the other boat to the lemonade stand. In the meantime, Lila will go by foot to the ice-cream parlor.

Solution on page 73

Want some help in making sense of the signposts? The tip is "codeword icecream"

Colorful Connection

Find the odd one out! If you are having trouble, the title of this puzzle might give you a clue. Or is it a red herring?

Solution on page 70

Time limit: 30 seconds.　　**Time limit:** 20 seconds.

6. Garbage Retrieval

"Isn't it terrible what people still throw away," said Lila. "You'd think they'd never heard of recycling or composting."

"Well, I must admit I recently threw away a red coat hanger just because I didn't like its color," confessed Tom.

"Shame on you!" exclaimed Lila.

"Go and find it again! And Ben, have you recently thrown away something as well? Something you shouldn't have?"

"Well, I did throw a boomerang . . ." Ben admitted sheepishly.

"Didn't it come back? Did you follow the instructions?"

"They were in a foreign language."

"Oh, I see," Lila replied, "Well, get those things back while I dash across the dumpsite to retrieve my backpack. But you must stay on the wooden boards. These dumpsites can be treacherous."

Solution on page 73

A boomerang should be the easiest thing to recycle!

Each of us will take a different entrance. Let's see where we'll meet up inside!

Conny thinks you'll never meet up!

17

7. Go Fly a Kite

Flying kites is a lot of fun, but not when they get stuck in a tree like this!

"Stay where you are!" cries the owner of the garden. "I don't want you to damage my precious Himalayan Spine Tree. Just tell me which kite is yours and I'll get it for you."

Can you work out the owner of each kite?

Solution on page 73

Imagine building a nest among those spines!

A Quiet Sunday Stroll to the Park . . .

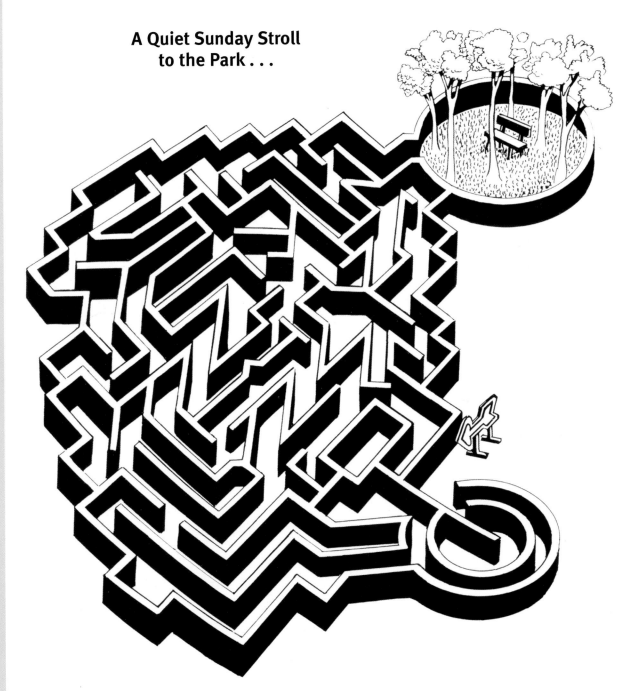

Telling Tails

Can you work out the length of each creature's tail?

My tail is 3 times longer than that of my cat. If it were 3.9 in. longer, it would be twice the size of yours. And if my cat's tail were 3.9 in. shorter, it would be half yours...

Answer on page 70

Horseshoe Shuffle

Kalamari has passed Foxtrotter and is in the lead while Wild Beauty has slipped to the rear. Hurricane is now positioned between Midnight and Foxtrotter. Which horse is second last?

Answer on page 70

8.   Challenging Chambers

At first glance, this job really looks hard. The children have to take the pegs from the center tower and fit them through the holes in the chambers until they reach the bottom.

But Lila soon finds that it's not as difficult as it looks. The objects in the chambers are a good guide.

Lila takes the round peg through the chambers that have an object starting with C—"C" for "Circle."

Tom discovers that the star-shaped peg goes through the chambers that have objects starting with S.

"I can't spell!" cries Ben. But that doesn't matter. He can still recognize the diamond-shaped holes through which to push his peg.

Solution on page 73

They start with "C" too! Look out for them in "Challenging Chambers"!

9. Lasseter's Reef

Harold Lasseter claimed in 1929 to have discovered a rich "reef of gold" in the region on the border between Western and Central Australia, but couldn't find it when he returned to the region. Well, Lasseter's gold reef has been rediscovered!

But it's not so easy to get there through the maze of mine shafts and tunnels. Lila, Tom, and Ben have each staked a claim.

Solution on page 74

Dazzling Duet II

Here are two more mazes.
See if you can find your way through both in under 90 seconds.

10.   Log Jam

Ben will take the red canoe and find a path through the floating logs to Middle Island, where Uncle Alf is chopping down the last three trees.

Tom will take the blue canoe and bring some dry socks to Uncle Joe.

There is no canoe left for Lila. She will have to walk over the logs to Rocky Island to tell the men they're wanted on the telephone.

Solution on page 74

Watch Your Step!

Make your way down by stepping only on the objects that are made of wood.

Solution on page 70

25

11. Tracks in the Snow

It is winter and the snow is full of tracks.

"Look!" cries Ben. "A rabbit went past here. Let's follow the paw prints and find out where it went!"

"Never mind the rabbit," says Tom. "Somebody took the nose from our snowman. And the rascal's footprints are still in the snow—let's follow them and find out who he is!"

"I don't want to waste my time on that," says Lila. "I'm following these ski tracks here. They're from my friend Elisa and I want to find out where she went."

Solution on page 74

Brrr... Too cold for me. Conny says winter is for the birds..

One-Minute Mazes!

Time yourself
—under one minute per maze: marvelous
—under two minutes: moderate
—over two minutes: miserable!

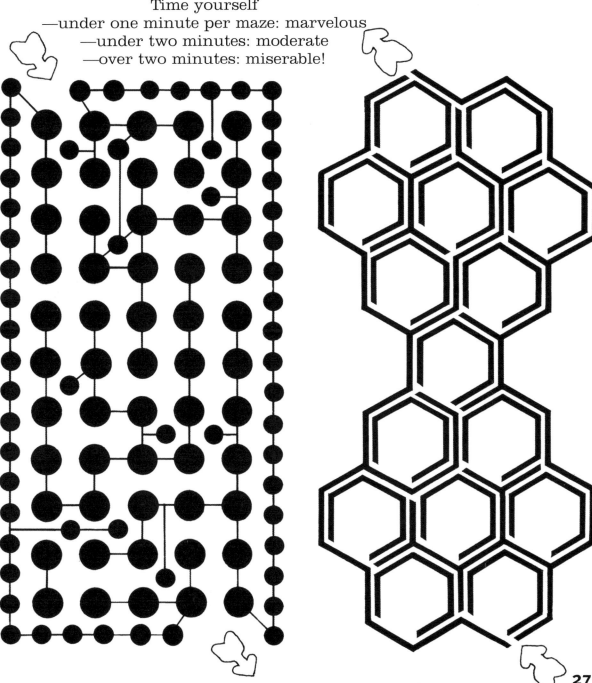

27

Alphabet Aerobics

Step from A to Z through the entire alphabet.
For example, start on A, then move to the Book for B,
then to the Cup for C, and so on.

Solution on page 70

12.　　　　　**Fruitful Quest**

Lila wants to pick some cherries, Tom will get the plums, and Ben the lemons. They should have a lot of fun finding their way to the fruit trees.

Ben will be guided by the sign of the lemons. Tom, if he keeps his eyes open, will find the whole alphabet on the way. Lila has the longest path, but if she's smart enough she will discover an encouraging message as she goes.

Solution on page 74

13. Half and Half

"This maze looks much too difficult for me," said Ben.

"Maybe it is," agreed Lila, "so here is a hint for you: turn right eight times. After that, you're on your own. Tom, you go with him. When you reach the top, it's you who has to lead the way back—but not the same way! You have to come back through the other half. And let me tell you—the two halves are not quite the same."

"What are you going to do?" Ben asked Lila.

"I'm going to put up that ladder and search for the three spots which make the left half different from the right half."

Solution on page 75

Ben will always take the easiest maze, Lila the hardest and Tom the one in between.

Did you know that even blind people can find their way through a maze if they stick to a simple rule? If your left hand always stays in touch with the left wall (or your right hand with the right wall) you can be sure to end up at the exit. It may take a long time, but at least you can't get lost forever. Try it!

Only one of the entrances leads to the tower. Can you find it?

14. Snail Trails

There's been a disaster at the International Snail Research Center! Who would have believed that the snails would be strong enough to break out? There were three kinds: the Californian Pink Foot, the Tasmanian Wriggle Tail, and the Nanasato Green. Luckily, they left their trails behind so that they can be traced. This is the children's job. Lila will try to collect all the Wriggle Tails, Tom the Pink Foots, and Ben the Nanasato Greens.

Only one of the entrances leads to the tower. Can you find it?

Solution on page 75

33

15. Frozen Footpaths

"I think the ice is breaking up," said Lila. "We had better get back to the boat. Ben, take the shortest route back, and Tom, you collect our picnic basket. I'm going back ashore to close the door of the Nissen hut. Someone forgot to close it. I'll meet you back on the ship!"

Solution on page 75

Don't you just love their suits!

The water seems to be rising!

Let's find the highest spot!

Rising Tide

Solution on page 70

Time limit: 30 seconds.

Time limit: 20 seconds.

Time limit: 30 seconds.

Time limit: 20 seconds.

16. Calamitous Contraption

Will it work? That depends not only on the specially bred Madagascan Malstock Beast, but on how well the children can operate the contraption. Ben will apply the brakes, but will he have to pull the lever up or down? And which way does Tom turn the wheel to lower the carrot? It is Lila's job to find out whether the vehicle will move backwards or forwards once it is in motion.

Solution on page 75

17. Coconut Confusion

Ben, Tom, and Lila went to visit their friends in Samoa. Lila will help guide Uncle Tufia's canoe through the coral reefs so that he can deliver his fresh coconuts to the ship. Tom wants to come along too. "I'm afraid not," said Uncle Tufia. "The boat is already overloaded, but we will give you a lift on the way back."

Solution on page 76

Stepping Stones

Make your way from top to bottom by following these rules:

 Stone can blunt scissors

 Scissors can cut paper

 Water can extinguish fire

 Paper can wrap stone

 Fire can burn paper

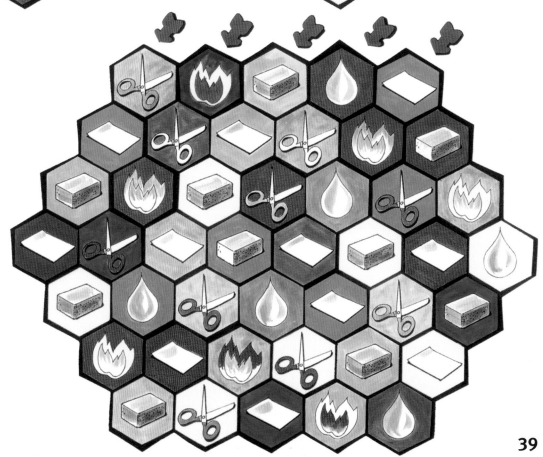

Final Feast

If you don't want to eat the spaghetti with your fingers, get
yourself a fork and spoon.

18. Lost Property

"I don't know why," said Tom, "but this place gives me the creeps. I'm glad we're out of it."

"Bad news," laughed Lila. "You have to go back because I think you left your cap in there!"

Tom touched his head. "You're right! And it's my favorite red one. But what about you, Lila? It looks like you forgot your white socks. And Ben, haven't you lost one of your shoes? Come on, let's all go back and find the way to our lost property."

Solution on page 76

The Giant Malayan Butterflower
(Floribustus incredibus)

The nectar is sweetest right at the center of the flower,
so help the butterflies find their way to it.

Jug Test

Only two of these jugs are identical.
Which two are they?

Answer on page 71

19.   **Bothersome Berries**

This task may not seem all that difficult, but it's extremely important to get it right.

The problem is that these three different fruits look so much alike that they are easily mistaken for one another. Ben must find the Giant Blue Wobble Cherry (or Dulcinosa) which is excellent for use in Blue Forest cake. Then there is the Big Kibble Berry, an excellent natural remedy for toothache. It's botanical name is Gloriosis. Tom must identify that.

And finally there is the extremely dangerous Blue Devil's Apple (Obnoxia fatalis), so poisonous that Lila must remove it before anyone comes to harm.

Imagine what could happen if there was a mix-up!

Solution on page 76

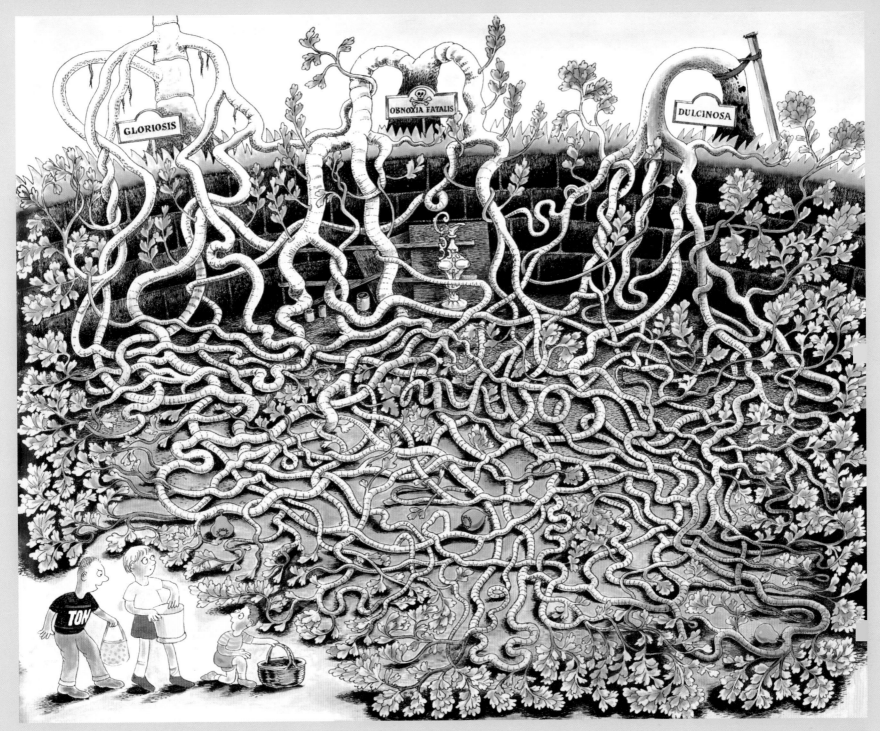

What is it that these images have in common?

Solution on page 71

Save the Beetle!

Time limit: 20 seconds.

20. Tangled Tubes

This waterslide into the hot springs looks like fun! Ben wants to splash into the hot pool, Tom likes the hotter one, and Lila would like to try the hottest. Now all they have to do is find their way through the right entrance and up to the correct starting platform.

Solution on page 76

HOT

HOTTER

HOTTEST

THE
RICHARD MILHOUSE
MEMORIAL
WATER SLIDE

21. Match and Swirl

"I like the look of that maze, but where do we have to go?" asked Tom.

"I think we'll know when we find our matching object!" said Lila. "Let's go!"

Solution on page 77

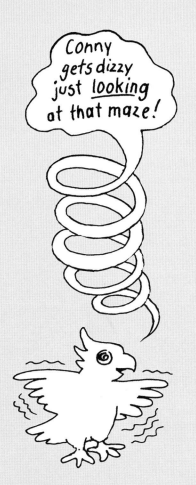

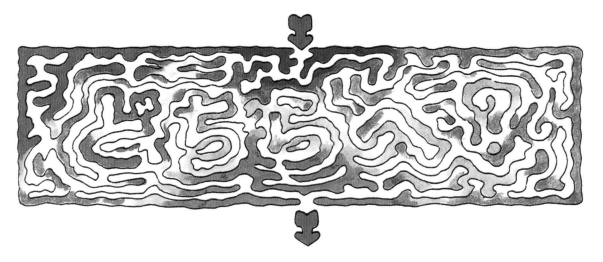

Time limit: 20 seconds.

Make your way to the center in less than 30 seconds!

47

Time limit: 20 seconds.
Good luck!

Barrel Boggle

Which barrel will fill with water?

You should be able to escape from the center in all four directions. By the way, the picture is not up the right way. To help you find north, south, east and west, there are the Japanese symbols for each compass point which can be matched to the shapes in the maze.

North   South   East   West

22.   Chow Chase

Ben, Tom, and Lila want to eat at their favorite restaurant in Bali, the famous Bamboo Palace. However, after the bridge was destroyed in a flood, it's not so easy to find the way. Lila will walk using any path, Tom will go by bicycle, which means that he can use any path except the ones with steps. Ben has decided to go by taxi, and he will show the driver which way to go. Let's hope there are no roadworks blocking the way!

Solution on page 77

49

23. Parceled Problems

Lila, Tom, and Ben have to make some urgent deliveries. Because the narrow lanes are so hard to get through, they find it easier to find a way over the rooftops. Can you help them to find the best way to deliver their parcels to the right owner?

Solution on page 77

24. Vexing Vine

Three minstrels have come to serenade the beautiful princess. Unfortunately, they do not know about the fast-growing vine. As dawn arrives, they find themselves shackled by the vine's tentacles. The only way to save the minstrels is to chop each plant off at the stem. Ben will save the bongo-drummer, Tom will save the alphorn horn player, and Lila will save the lutist.

Solution on page 77

Time limit: 30 seconds.

52

25. Moldy Maze

"Hey, what's with all the toadstools?" asked Tom.

Lila explained, "This is a very dangerous place. These toadstools were grown by the illustrator himself so that we'll fall on something soft if we should slip. He tried mattresses, but they were rather unsightly. Our task is to make a journey and come back to this very spot here without retracing our steps."

"Sounds easy," said Tom.

Lila wasn't so sure. Ben had to make his journey without stepping either up or down, Tom had to go down only, and Lila had to find a path stepping up only. Usually such a thing would have been impossible, but this place was built by a fan of Escher.

Ben is the youngest. He does the easiest mazes.

Tom is a little older, so his mazes are harder.

Lila, being the oldest of the three, does the hardest mazes of all.

Solution on page 78

Who is Escher anyway?

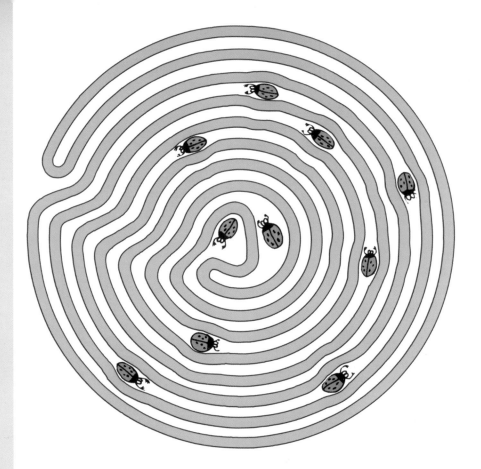

Beetlemania

Which of the beetles will be able to find their way out and which will stay trapped forever?

You'll only get dizzy following the tracks with your eyes. Here's a tip: Count the lines. An even number means freedom, an odd number means the beetles stay trapped.

Collector's Item

A major mistake has
been made in one of these stamps!

Answer on page 71

Hippy Group Photo 1975

Peachblossom was, as usual,
between Rain and Starlight.
Tango was then proudly
sporting an Afro hairstyle.
Jimini was wearing his
oversized Army pants.
Sunbeam, never without his
hat, was behind Rain and
Lightfoot. What was the name
of the guitar player?

Answer on page 71

56

26. Flagging Faces

"Why do I have the
feeling we're being
watched?" asked Ben.
"It's downright scary."

"You're right," agreed
Tom. "But you know,
once you find out just
what it is that makes you
scared, half your fear is
already gone. Let's find
all those hidden faces and
stare right back at them!"

"Good idea," agreed
Lila, "but first we must
do what we've been sent
to do. Exchange these
three flags with the old
ones of the same color
that have become a bit
tattered."

Solution on page 78

Let's face it, they can't face faces!

27. Domination

"Correct me if I'm wrong," said Ben, "but isn't there only one way to find a path over dominoes, and that is to have dominoes whose ends contain the same number of dots joined up together."

"Yes, that's the usual way," agreed Lila, "and you may use it to make your way to our teddy bear. But there are two other ways as well and they are a bit more difficult. Tom, you must step over the dominoes that are joined together and are the same color, and I have to step over the dominoes where the colors of the dots match. I'll see you at Teddy Bear Island!"

Solution on page 78

Would you believe there are 22 differences between the two Egyptian panels above?

Answer on page 71

Asp a silly question . . .
Can the asp escape?

59

General Confusion

Which of the four uniforms matches
that worn by General Sloan-Deppenkirk?

Answer on page 71

Mini-Mazes:

You should be able to
whiz through these
in 30 seconds flat!

28. Paint the Tower Red!

"Ah, blue and yellow!"
exclaimed Tom, "my
favorite colors!"

"Too bad," said Lila
"Our job is to paint the
tower red. Ben, you find
the paint and Tom, you
find a brush. Then both
of you have to get up the
stairs, any stairs, while
I stay on the ground and
make my way to the door
of the tower. I'll meet you
at the tower, okay?"

Solution on page 78

I hate to say it, but it seems an awful waste of time to build such huge mazes!

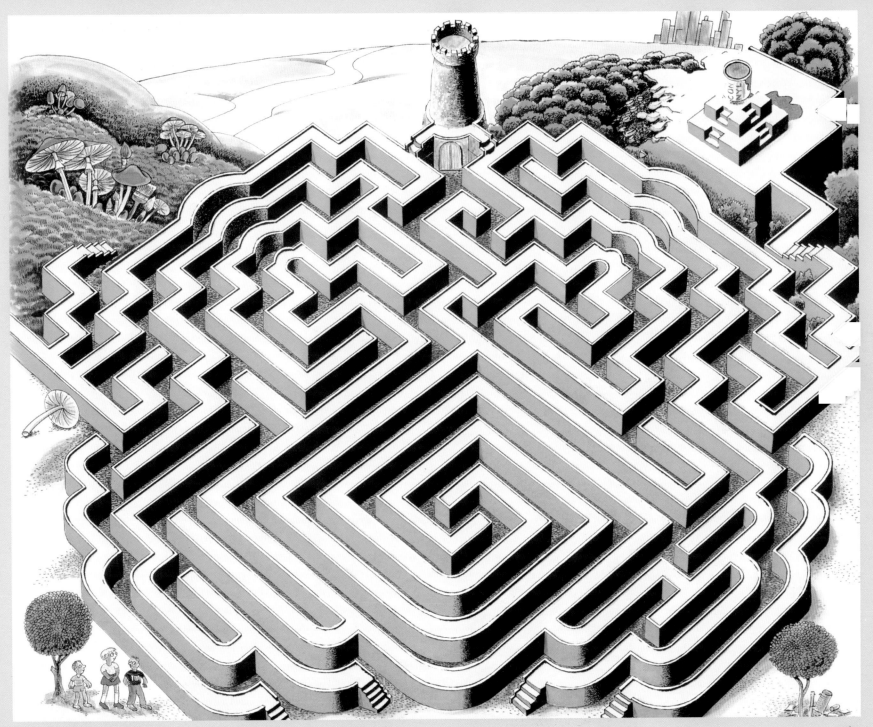

29. Problem Pets

The children have been told to feed the animals: Tom has a carrot for the rabbit, Lila has a bone for the dog, and Ben has some milk for the cat. Won't they get a surprise when they see the size of the animals!

Solution on page 79

Surveillance Photos

Detective Smart has been given these two surveillance photos. Although he has not been told which of the photos was taken earlier than the other, he knows straight away which one it was.

Answer on page 71

Star Express

Time limit: one minute

30. Curly Christmas

"Of all the weird places we've been in, this has to be the weirdest," exclaimed Tom. "What do we have to do here?"

"It's simple really," explained Lila. "We have to meet at the Christmas tree. Don't get dizzy on the way! Oh! And Merry Christmas!"

Solution on page 79

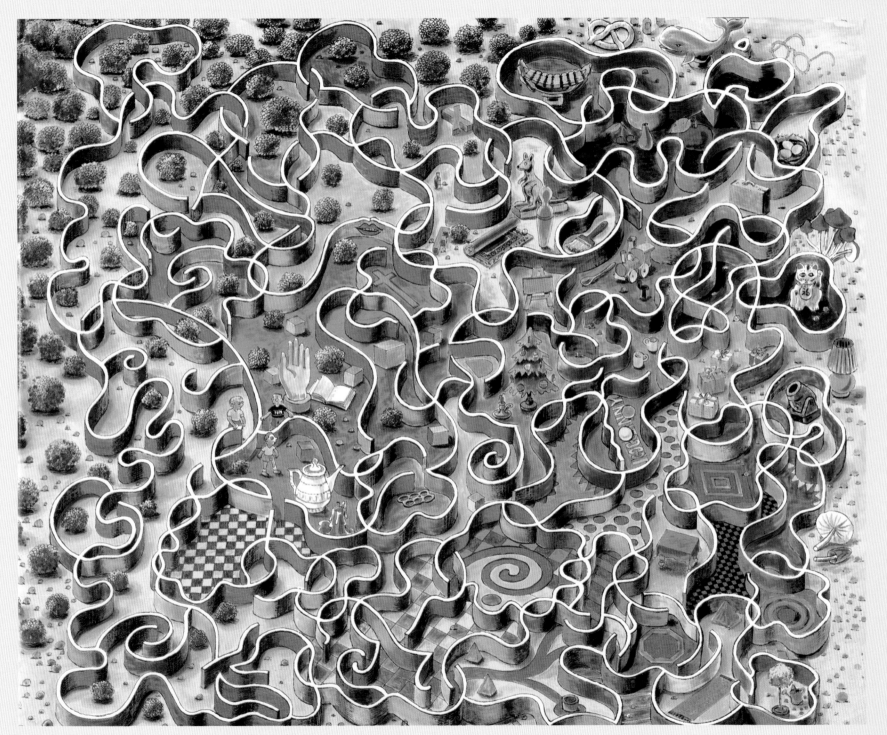

65

TOP SECRET

TOP SECRET

GO AWAY! THERE ARE NO ALIENS*

*IT'S JUST Swampgas or a weather balloon

TAPU
SECRETO
GEHEIM
SEGREDO
立入禁止
RAHASIA
RAHASYAM
GEHEEM · GO HOME
ПРЯТАТЬ
FAA SAINA · ALU ESE
TABOO

31. Alien Assignment

Lila, Tom, and Ben have made friends with an alien called Xotltoxox who came in search of his brother, Iboki. Iboki had been captured by the US Air Force and kept in a secret facility in New Mexico. "How are we going to get past the guards?" asked a worried Lila. "Easy," said Xotltoxox. "I know a secret spell that turns military guards into harmless ropossums for five minutes. Ropossums are native animals of my home planet, by the way. But five minutes is all we would have. While I watch the ropossums, you, Ben, find our six-legged space dog, Stripo. And Tom, you find the spacecraft, it looks exactly like mine. And Lila, could you look for my identical twin brother?"

"Oh, please, please, please," begged Ben, "please, please, please, please tell us that secret spell. It would be worth its weight in gold." "I can't do that," said Xotltoxox.

"A secret is a secret is a secret."

Solution on page 79

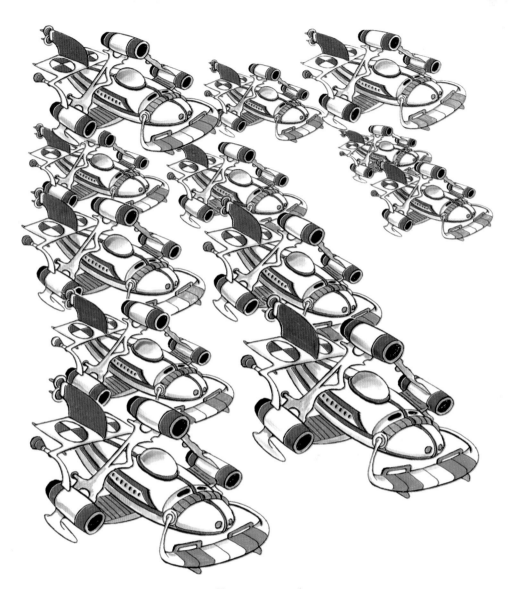

Starfleet Patrol

Eleven spaceships have set out to patrol the galaxy. Imagine the commander's surprise when he suddenly found there were twelve! An enemy ship has joined them; it is a clever replica. The enemy, however, made one mistake when building the replica which makes their ship easy to spot.

Answer on page 71

32. Timeout

"This place is called Kronopark because we have to find our way in chronological order," explained Lila. "Chronological order? I hope it isn't painful," said Ben, sounding a little concerned.

Lila laughed. "Chronological means arranged in the correct order according to the time in which something happened. Ben, you guide us on the right path, while Tom puts these names to the monuments they belong to. I'll put these signs with the year on the right spot. It'll be like a walk through history."

"Wait a minute," called Tom. "I've never heard of anyone called Carl Neanderthal!"

"Well," said Lila, "maybe that's Lesson Number One—never lose your sense of humor!"

Solution on page 71

Answer on page 71.

Lateral Thinking
Each panel has something in common with the picture on either side. To make it harder for you, the answer is written back to front!

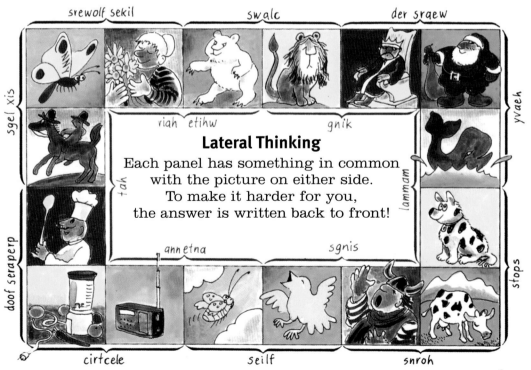

69

"Let's do an amazing experiment," suggested Tom.
"Both of us will keep our hands on the left-hand side wall and walk at the same speed until we come out again. When we meet each other, we'll call out and Lila will know we're exactly halfway through."
"Hmm, we'll see," said Lila. "Ready, set go!"

70

Solutions

PAGE 13. Cockatoo, owl, lark, kookaburra, albatross, sandpiper, robin. The codeword on the lower picture is SUNLIGHT.

PAGE 15. Colorful Connection: The hat is the odd one out. It is the only item that does not contain the color red.

PAGE 20. Telling Tails: The creature's tails are 59 inches (150 cm), 31.49 inches (80 cm), and 19.6 inches (50 cm) (the cat).

PAGE 20. Horseshoe Shuffle: The second last horse is Midnight.

PAGE 25. Watch Your Step!: Cradle, tree stump, chair, chest, log, table, tree, bowl, fence, gate.

PAGE 28. Alphabet Aerobics: A book, cup, drum, eye, flower, glasses, house, island, jar, kangaroo, leaf, matches, nose, octopus, pan, Queen, rope, scissors, television, unicorn, violin, water, xylophone, yellow, Z.

PAGE 35. Rising Tide:

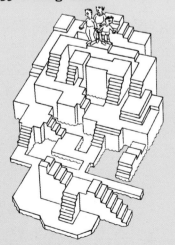

PAGE 42. Jug Test: Jugs 2 and 5 are identical.

PAGE 44. The images have the number 2 in common. Two eyes, two wheels, two birds, etc.

PAGE 56. Collector's Item: One of the stamps has a dollar sign instead of a cent sign.

PAGE 56. Hippy Group Photo 1975: Lightfoot is the guitar player.

PAGE 59: Egyptian Panels:

PAGE 60. General Confusion: The uniform left bottom.

PAGE 63. Surveillance Photo: Detective Smart knew that the photo on the right was taken earlier—the trees in the photo on the left are taller and more plaster has fallen off the wall.

PAGE 67. Starfleet Patrol: The top left space ship has a mirror-reversed tail design.

PAGE 68. Timeout: This is the path through, in chronological order:

1. CLUB. Neanderthalers lived about 70,000 years ago, but their more primitive ancestors had already used such simple tools.

2. OAR. Oars found in Denmark have been dated to 7,000 BC.

3. WHEEL. Wheels were used in Sumer in about 3,500 BC. Rollers had been used before.

4. WRITING. In about 2,200 BC, the Minoans used pen and ink for linear writing. Other methods had been used before.

5. COMPASS. Magnetic needles were probably used in China in 1,115 BC.

6. WINDMILL. About 700 BC.

7. PRINTING. Gutenberg was the first European to use moveable type in about 1455.

8. MICROSCOPE. The Romans had already used glass balls filled with water as magnifying glasses, but in the 17th Century, Antonie van Leeuwenhoek and others pioneered the building of a proper microscope.

9. BALLOON. In 1783 the Montgolfier brothers, French aeronautical inventors, staged the first manned hot-air balloon flight.

10. STEAM LOCOMOTIVE. In 1804, Richard Trevithick, a British inventor, built the first self-propelled locomotive. (George Stephenson's railway opened in 1825.)

11. PHOTOGRAPHY. In 1826, Joseph Nicéphore Niépce made the first photograph. It took eight hours to expose!

12. TELEGRAPH. Alexander Graham Bell patented the telephone in 1876.

13. PENNY FARTHING. The penny farthing, an early model of bicycle, was invented by James Starley in 1871.

14. TELEPHONE. Alexander Graham Bell patented the telephone in 1876.

15. ELECTRIC LAMP. Patented by Thomas Edison in 1879.

16. CAR. The first successful gas-driven car was invented in 1885 by Karl Friedrich Benz.

17. X-RAYS. Discovered in 1895 by Wilhelm Conrad Roentgen.

18. CINEMA. In 1895, the Lumière brothers made improvements on photographic equipment and patented the cinematograph.

19. RADIO. Patented in 1896 by Guglielmo Marconi.

20. PLANE. The Wright brothers made the first motorized flight in 1903.

21. TELEVISION. In 1924, John Logie Baird transmitted the first television pictures.

22. SATELLITES. The first manmade satellite was the Sputnik, sent into orbit by the Russians in 1957.

23. MOON WALK. In 1969, Neil Armstrong and Edwin Aldrin were the first men to walk on the moon.

24. PERSONAL COMPUTERS. Having been improved over a number of decades, computers came into wider use in the 1970s.

PAGE 69. The Martians will win.

1. The Labyrinth

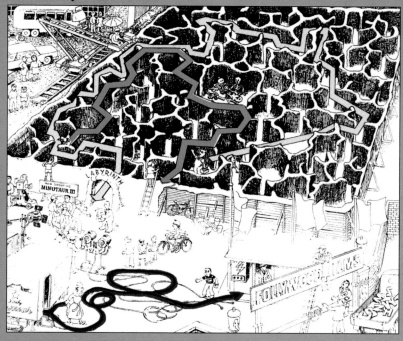

2. Drinks in the Pipeline

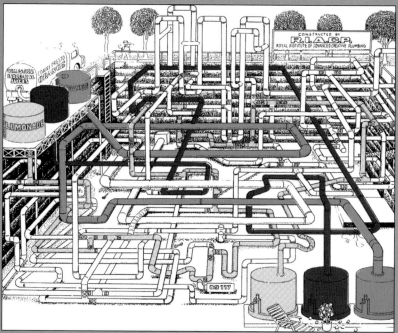

3. Professor McQueen's Breakfast Machine

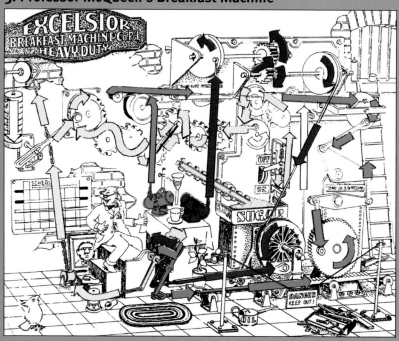

4. Matching Socks

5. Puzzling Picnic

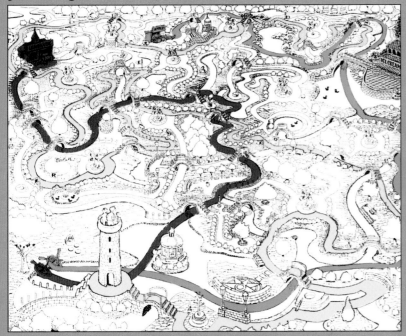

6. Garbage Retrieval

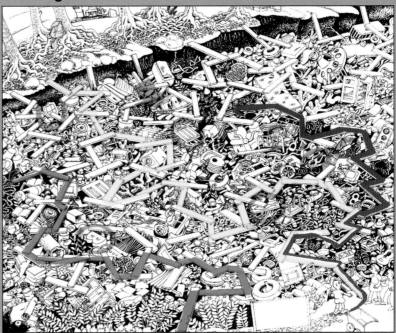

7. Go Fly a Kite

8. Challenging Chambers

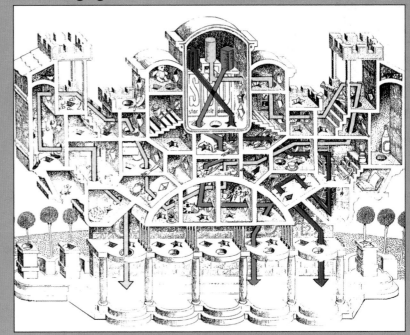

9. Lasseter's Reef

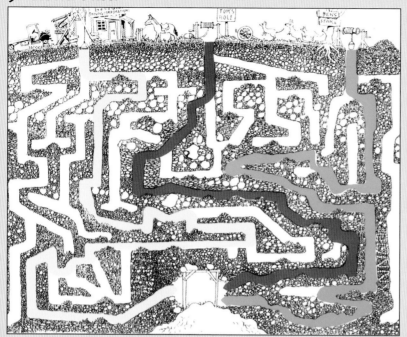

10. Log Jam

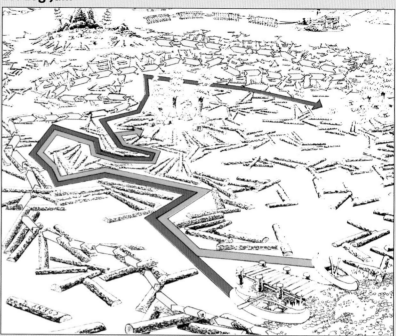

11. Tracks in the Snow

Ben = Red   Tom = Pink   Lila = Yellow

12. Fruitful Quest

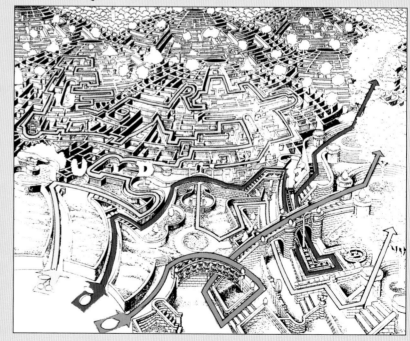

Lila's encouraging message was: You are doing well! Congratulations

13. Half and Half

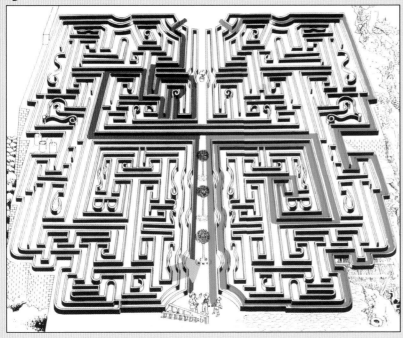

14. Snail Trails

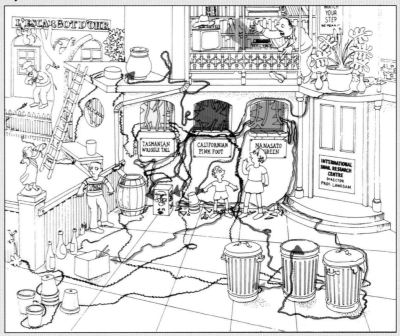

15. Frozen Footpaths

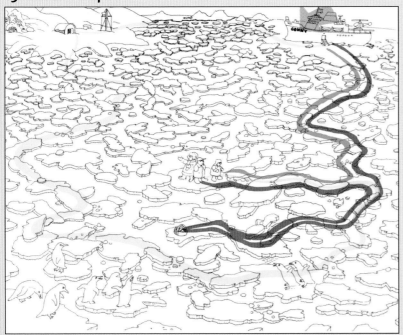

16. Calamitous Contraption

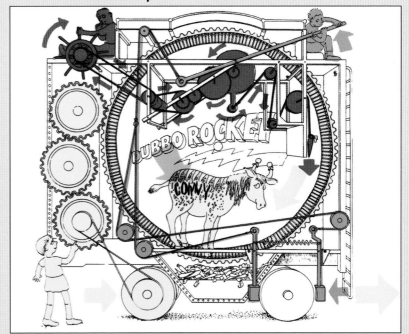

Green arrow - Connie's name

17. Coconut Confusion

18. Lost Property

19. Bothersome Berries

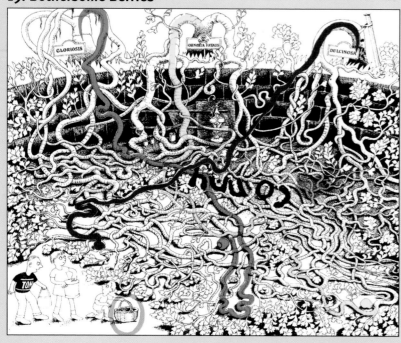

20. Tangled Tubes

Ben = Pink   Tom = Blue   Lila = Yellow

21. Match and Swirl

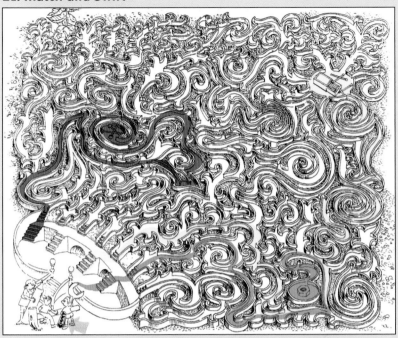

22. Chow Chase

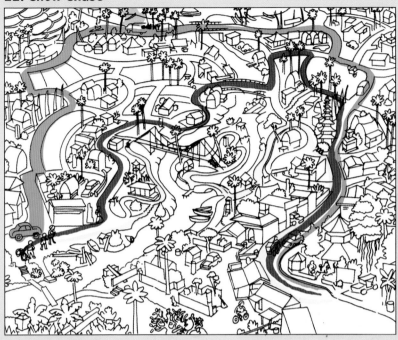

23. Parceled Problems

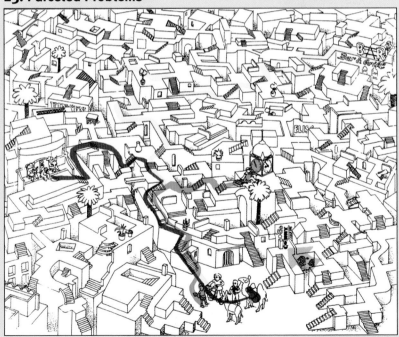

24. Vexing Vine

25. Moldy Maze

26. Flagging Faces

27. Domination

28. Paint the Tower Red!

Ben = Pink   Tom = Blue   Lila = Yellow

29. Problem Pets

30. Curly Christmas

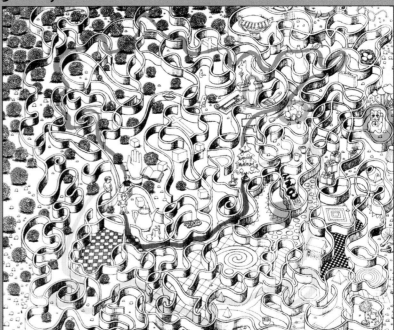

31. Alien Assignment

Ben = Pink   Tom = Blue   Lila = Yellow

Index